HER WOMANHOOD OF MINE

HER WOMANHOOD OF MINE

POEMS

Haley Hutchinson

GREEN WRITERS PRESS
Brattleboro, Vermont

Printed in the United States

10 9 8 7 6 5 4 3 2 1

Green Writers Press is a Vermont-based publisher whose mission is to spread a message of hope and renewal through the words and images we publish. Throughout we will adhere to our commitment to preserving and protecting the natural resources of the earth. To that end, a percentage of our proceeds will be donated to environmental activist groups. Green Writers Press gratefully acknowledges support from individual donors, friends, and readers to help support the environment and our publishing initiative.

Green Writers Press

Giving Voice to Writers & Artists Who Will Make the World a Better Place

Green Writers Press | Brattleboro, Vermont

www.greenwriterspress.com

ISBN: 979-8-9923988-9-2

Printed on 100% PCW recycled paper by Bookmobile.
Based in Minneapolis, Minnesota, Bookmobile began as a design and typesetting production house in 1982, and started offering print services in 1996.
Bookmobile is run on 100% wind- and solar-powered clean energy.

For her, always.

Apricots the size of marbles
fell into our mouths that summer.
We took ginger steps beneath their shadow,
careful to not squish the fallen.
The upside-down cake above us
green, then ripe, always full
of promise.

Contents

Part II

Pleasant Street

Part III

Pierce Street

Resolutions

1
The only way to make somebody whole
is to fill them with something
they do not already know.

2
When the world splits in two
halves of stone fruit, yours will hold
the side nestled by wooded pit, mine —
hollowed by the weight
of some unspoken machinery.

3
Count days back and
froth at the mouth only to learn
you made peace with it all, this unholy,
a long time ago.

4
Notice the small and become
something out of it.

5
Cumin and eggs, burning softly,
infiltrate the new days of September. Let their scent
stain our sheets for free.

6
Please, let me cry when the good part starts
and savor the snug fit of heads on chests and
ginger tea teasing the throat.

7
Tell me this is not
what you thought living was and then live
a little more, a lot longer — please, let this
be the rest of time.

8
Sit in a window seat and rest your memory on the
cold, hard plastic. Romanticize the depression
of leaving lost love on the ground as you fly, lost
and alone and beautiful, back to a place shaped
to the contours of your insides, all along.

9
Be practical when it counts but save dreaming
for the softest parts of you — the skin of your
wrist, the inch behind your ear, the stretch
of your stomach.

10
Learn to love your stomach.

11
Existing seasonally means there never comes
a time when you can't learn to breathe, anew.

12
Become an atlas of wintering and bloom-
ing and falling over and again until
an ending is obsolete.

13
Fall asleep and imagine the wet curtains
of your eyelids, dancing.

Part I

PINE STREET

Girlhoods

Make me the girl
holed up
in the tree
on the left side
heading west
gravel washed out and rutted, make me
the ruddy-cheeked rose between her lips
the blood that comes with her smile
open and wanting then leave me
wanting. Make me the girl
in the corner
at the party
the girl I never kissed, the girl
with straight black hair an angle
to her chin bring me
the coolness of her shoulder, bring me
the girl with shoulders
showing, summertime simple pleasures, always
something to be said for the girl
in a sundress, I know it
because I was one, once, back when
a part of me wanted to be made
by your looking, back when I wanted
at all.

I missed
what it felt like to be needed.
I needed to be felt
like winter wool pierced into something whole:
Ornament. Pillow. Pocket
to remember my bones by.

I wondered how much sand my mouth could hold
before it turned back to rock. I put tomatoes
to my tongue and tasted nothing. The seeds stuck
between my teeth, the slime irritated my gums
and that was all.

When I was unwanting, I took caution with nothing.
Bodies, without. Words like leeches, begging
for a warm knot to call, sentence.
The sidewalk squished beneath me. I forgot
where I was going. I never knew
where I was going.

The girls: My footsteps
coating cement and snow.
The girls: Priming marble ballrooms and
pine needle glens.
The girls I wanted to become.
The girls I never was.
The girls I was, once.
To the girl I am now:

Become a circle of blood orange and savor the sweet
but remember the bitter. Kiss
when it counts. Sprawl in spring lupine and
forget-me-nots and taste the color of purple
like an old friend, like the pit of coming
home late at night and feeling twelve years ago, deeply.
Touch your skin to the grass and don't hesitate
when you look at the sky straight on.

Until the Morning

Forgive me.

These dispersed tears were not the wine
left splattered on your stained table. The table
that sang notes of must, if you got close enough.
These tears they pooled
into the watershed of your palm
mapping veins of salty warmth full
of ions too charged
to talk about. Forgive me
for that, too — the not talking
the not holding your hand between my own
skin and sweat; forgive me, for not having
the words and only
the tears.

On the chipped windowsill,
a salt-shaker vase sits
perched and warped, holding
clipped *Cécile Brünner* roses — their sweetness
still, patient, pressed in velvet knots.
I am waiting for their presence
to seep slowly, their scent,
their time.

When the sun comes up we are told it is novel.
Mornings fresh, the wine in the fridge, eyes dry and bruised,
our hands untangled and cracking. The roses on the sill,
opening. Forgive me for trusting
in the telling of time by way of floral arrangements,
for seeking solace in all their bloomed bounty and passing.

This evening the roses hang drying like bats,
as aged as expensive cheese.
The wrinkled roses hang, accumulating forgiveness.
I am the rose on your table,
the sun blushing the room
in streaks of yesterday.

To the Kitchen, for Filling

Torn basil
          and cubed crisp melon
I place upon a wooden cutting board.
Their separate piles complimentary
          in their greenness —
one's algal luster
the other, the sliver of sun
teasing a clear ocean horizon
the millimetric second
          the flash —
          to see it twice would be lucky,
          not impossible.

In the morning, cages of
          spider web crochet hang
strung among aster, yarrow —
          in the entropy
I seek pattern, a grid
that could place me
          a coordinate
on its axis. Three

canvas totes hang
on the pantry door handle, each
          softer with every use.
Grocery lists forgotten
          or completed
accumulate in their bellies.

These days I prefer to eat
          with chopsticks

slow and savored spice —
the last bead of brown rice
waits at the bottom of the bowl
patient.

November is well-plated
like a persimmon sliced
into topaz eclipses —
plush and crunch, a single bite
the orange flesh
lingering with the afterthought
of winter.

Her Womanhood of Mine

Tell me it is mother like daughter. String me up in Edison
bulb parade, this carefully measured backyard trigonometry,
this home you angle with corners of bright.

Let me sit in your nest of used feathers until they prickle
from my back, my vertebrae rounded and unfurling,
mimosa pudica in reverse.

Feed me your soil, your skin cells evaporating
500 million each day, a garnish I taste off your thumb
printed on my lip.

Your molting is my maturing. I am your bird
and you, my love for life. This earth made damp from your sweat,
this first blink of winter sun

fingernailing over the fence, its warmth,
your babushka embrace, and my broken shells
like fallen confetti I bury beneath us.

Driveway, 35 miles

In the backseat, I am holding on
to a fistful of rust.
The window is murky,
painted and primed with
ageless highway debris, refined
and recoated. Every mile
another layer, making it hard
to distinguish
between grit and tint.

My molars grind
with each tar-turned switch-
back, the teeth
who never outgrew their ridges.
Better that way for chewing the reeds
ribboning the pond, the reeds
all vibrant green and coffee-ground brown,
acrylic swords of summer.
The reeds cracking and tanned, ugly
in February, much like the screeching cry
of two elementary school lips,
a clarinet,
and the blue glare
of auditorium lighting.

The good-bye, the return, always
such pain without practice.

November of Earlier

Thanksgiving, too early for gingerbread
but you and I walked from the snow-piled house
to see the houses built from molasses and grit.
There was something wrong, a reason why
the lead in my arms made me long for your torso
on mine, two curled ribbons of softened onion
warming in a cast iron, even though
your hand cupped mine and you
were there. Winter has always
accompanied loneliness despite closer quarters
made lustrous with swirls of nutmeg and
hearth, that warmth that leaves me wanting.

They Say I Look Just Like You

I.

You were born in September
Orange, New Jersey. Green, your color. Daffodil, the house.

You learned to swim in the Atlantic, small and hourglassed,
they say I look just like you.

Your best friend, Bobby, taught you how to laugh.
I wonder who I would have been if you'd married him, how
you would have sounded.

Instead, a young man from an Idahoan Mormon family waited
on you:
It was Columbia, New York City, 1957, the charm.

1958, you married,
fell in line with his life — Missouri, New Mexico, Arizona,
Doctor.

You made a home in the foothills of desert, carved of adobe.
Two girls, two towns, some years.

You hosted Christmas Eve parties, served patient smiles
on platters, domestic tokens from your mother-in-law.

You lived with quiet because that was simple, safe in holy
matrimony.
How deeply did you bury your dreams?

I know you stowed them under layers of sandy soil where
they slept in a garden you wanted that soon became a botanica
of his direction.

You adapted to the desert aridity, you blame the times, not
your will.
Your skin quickly olived and wrinkled.

I know you missed the ocean, heavy air and salt.
You settled with chlorine kisses from the racquet club pool.

You've been retired for decades, but he still sets a 5am alarm,
your day is complete before it starts.

You fill the warmer hours with black and white
prints, make art from a past you never had.

II.

You don't sleep anymore
so you find night in the darkroom at 2pm.

It used to be a closet filled with mops, now it secretes
imaginary history
framed by pinhole cameras and red light.

You capture moments and cut them out, rearrange
their pieces in disarray, finding narratives more suitable.

Who knew black and white could hold such color, but you fill
silhouettes with life, histories of intimacies.

Your body stands over the sink
and washes away the film residue, you never know what
  you'll get.

III.

I know twenty-three percent of your lifetime.
I know the dry musk of the adobe house, your maiden name.

I feel your weather-worn fingers splicing paper
  at the white table,
your voice in the red-accented living room.

I want to know you
tending to your garden, rain-soaked from the recent
  monsoons.

I watch your small frame from the kitchen window,
  unearthing the soil,
pulling up root matrices.

In the heat of September
you go to the nursery to get geraniums, poinsettia red.

IV.

We sat in your car, the white paint doing nothing to
  keep the heat out
from the crinkled asphalt below.

I asked you that day about love, and you wished you'd known.
Maybe it was the time, or the man, or the obligation.

It was eighty-five years, you were twenty.
Years aligned as matches in the box, sixty-five count.
Now I search for matches to light the fireplace in the middle
  of summer.
We search for small comforts.

V.

Because he does not know the difference
between May and December, Christmas comes early.

He does not understand the sharpness of his weight you carry
digging into the nape of your neck.

He never had a taste for cooked greens
but now is more confident in his disgust. We call it loss
  of etiquette.

The day will come when he forgets your name, but even then
you will stay.

VI.

I link my elbow in yours at the mailbox.
We walk the mile loop you could do in your sleep, but I like
  to hold you.

The sun beats and beads on my head, the backs of our legs.
Your hand cool in mine.

I take two steps for every four of yours.
Via Entrada, Soledad, Foothill Drive then gravel.

When the desert sky darkens, the air does too, but not enough
to gift us sleep.

So I mold next to you on the egg-speckled couch,
spoons of chocolate ice cream, melting in the stillness.

Tomato Dreams

Late October and thinking about tomatoes,
ruby plush ornaments all heavy and eager
on fallen green fingers —
How the briny scent of plucked stems fills
low afternoon light, the corner of the backyard made ours
in the relish we make of this prized feast.
In May, the market opens on Franklin Street.
Late spring too early for tomatoes but still we wish with closed
lips to see the early girls heaped in wooden crates,
the ones we will select gingerly and fill two
brown paper sacks with. We will be patient
for summertime. But in October, I'm still thinking about tomatoes
and early summer and their smell and squish
and I'm thinking of our coupled feet-falls splattering
up Pine, after school, that time of day when these five blocks
of mismatched concrete could be
the whole world.

Nights Spent in the Paper House

You have taught me how
to exact my words, splice
with the plastic orange razor blade
you use to finesse
the edges of paper,
gold-embossed
& checkered, red & turmeric,
the paper patch-worked
around the adobe studio.
You taught me the art
of deconstruction; I learned
both breakage & beauty
begin with the letter *b*. Be
patient, you tell me, my words,
like your hands, will age and crack
in the dry desert air then soften,
into something worth it all.
Your small touch
on the nape of my neck is familiar.
Goodnight, I tell you from the doorway,
the yellow glow of the lamp
still illuminating the adobe room
long after I close my eyes, your hands
still slicing & pasting, creating
new words, new quilts you wrap
yourself into, this village of paper
houses bright & calculated where
you rest for the night, or was it
a lifetime?

Triangular Conventions

I.

I was taught to fold
in on myself

corner
to
  corner

a square-turned-triangle

like the peanut butter and honey
pasted between wheat bread,
the flavor of growing pains,
first left for me
on a kitchen counter,
late afternoon,
then later, older,
the indulgence
of my own making.

The nutty sweetness
always tasted better
cut tri-laterally,
three neat sides, the crusts
staling in coastal air.
In the kitchen, unquestioning,
I learned the lessons of trigonometry,
found comfort
in straightness and
whole grain regularity:

the evening
the folding
the clean lines
the triangles
unfaltering.

Now grown, I am
watching the triangles
of my years secured
by three corners,
three sides,
accumulate, a noiseless heap
in the corner
of an old room.

The room
with its walls. The walls
with their paper prints,
atrocious patterns fading,
peeling, replaced each year.

The walls'
evolving uglinesses
always watching

the triangles — my life

kept neatly, savored
just in case
it all meant
anything.

II.

The porcelain points are
untouched by the graying,
aging room. Over
and over I was told to fold,
heard whispered reminders
of the perfection
of the number three —
safe, un-strayable,
Countable.

I wonder now:

When will I fracture?

I see the triangles
in the corner
like shattered plates,
the clanking of poker chips,
shards of whiskey-
stained glass,
clean lines left broken, soiled.

I wonder now:

Was the geometric precision regrettable,
calculations forgettable,
underwhelming at best?

When will I remember
three is an odd
number, divisible by
nothing
but itself —

Cautions to Consider When Playing Pretend

In this disguise
I lose sight

of the inside. Some
would say that is the point

of dress-up, like when we were kids
rummaging through a red plastic bin —

we did not know we were playing
pretend.

These days I wonder if I am still —
pastel chiffon

the blue and pink, artificial gems
scratchy on our skin

replaced with a graying face,
mossing bones,

the damp smell only noticeable
when I forget myself,

when the proximity
of what [is] and what [could]

is too much, the air
too crusted to bear.

The shadows under my eyelids
nothing but cloud cover

reflected
by the Midnight pool

the wayside puddle, still
before the rain,

the en-circadian midpoint
when it all could work.

I tell myself this
down the darkened hall

but the bathroom mirror
catches my face before my breath,

and risked hope leaves me tapping
on silver glass, waiting for anything.

Valentine's Day

My affinity for soft
sheep cheese
and jam
came later, years
after the February fourteenths spent
in the stale afternoon-warmed rooms
of elementary classes,
licking the sticky goo
from grimy fingers.
I pretended
to enjoy the flavor
because of how pretty
they looked.
The white and
red spread
on the precarious platform
of a heart-shaped water cracker.
How elegant
they were laid
on germ encrusted desks
next to Pepto-Bismol
lollipops, plasticky
chocolate wrapped
in crinkled foil knocking
on the faux wood. I relish
now the sweet
tang of goat cheese and figs
smeared on sourdough
washed down with dry wine,
a taste acquired.
I should be thanking you
for every tooth
of mine you sprouted.

Dear Mama,

You braided me with your hands
and left your fingers to grow from my wrists
so when they ask me who my mother is, I say
look at me face-up. They'll no longer wonder

who baked this bread.

//

Did you know I spent the entire month of March
tracing lazy spirals, contemplating my 9-month sublet

until you heard my knocking and I was made
to stay. I slow-cooked down, curves like the sticky
-sweet of caramelized onion and plump
like a raisin in warm water until

summer ended. And I needed air.

//

I waited until October because
the seventh day of the month tastes like fresh rust
and smells mashed orange and earthy from the soil

and I wanted to be the kind of life
that is sweet and sacred.

//

I want to know what I smelled like
when you lifted me to your face. Was it pungent and organic;
was it red? I want to know the metric of your inhale
and exhales the night I took my first breath, doused

in pink and yellow slime, hospital sheets wet
with the sweat of your strain.

//

Did you cry tears the size of lemon seeds
when my mossy form finally emerged,
were the tears of relief or disbelief,

snot dribbling from your nose?
The stale air, your eyes blue and wet
and mine brown like chestnuts.

//

I want to know your firsts, if they were anything
like mine. Even now
I am still waiting to find my feet in your steps.

I follow their crinkle-cut pattern,
I walk and walk until I feel myself getting warmer,
until desert nights fill my lungs.

//

I want to know you,
sitting shrouded by late afternoon,
in a plum chair that refuses to be discarded,

when steam smelling of ginger root, lemon rind,
and spice clouds the inches between
your nose and a book, its pages long since foxed.

//

And Mama,

I want to know you
when the December rain sobs on a Friday evening,
when red lentils boil in hearty matrimony
with generous chunks of tomato and garlic,
you at the stove, breath at the window,
four bowls lightly chipped

waiting patiently on the table.

//

What We Take with Us

Beale Lane.

The back step coated with bits of dead pampas grass and sand.
Where the bitterness of the wine spilling over my small
  shoulders kept me
warm. I clung to Papa's torso as the garnet bled
onto a favorite tee — the orange one
with the butterfly patch on the chest.
Where I learned about the fleeting
pulse of inebriation and other adult matters.

AM Run.

The grow room on Pleasant St, its fuschia glow. Its curtains
now tightly drawn, shutting out the world and all our wanting.
The family who lives inside. Their simple dinners. A wood
  burning stove.
If they pray, I want their hands
to know pink is my favorite color, too.

We'll Get Back to You.

On the answering machine we count the blinking messages,
bright ruby numbers illuminating the dark office. Every year
they tock down — 12, 8, 3 — as fewer people feel the need
to get in touch with us. Hardly anybody has a landline now, but I
still remember the digits of elementary school
  friends' phone numbers,
the sharp curves of seven digits, all nines and sixes and ones.
I don't recall the color of their eyes.

Salt Town.

Our houses were wooden there, surrounded by strips of brown, gray,
green. Our homes, built from the living to hold our breathing. Our laughing.
Our loving. The windows sweaty with the residue of salty breath,
the air mixed with our own.

Bricks.

I am 3,000 miles away, and there is less salt. My existence is cornered off
by red rectangles, crumby bits piled into storefronts, apartments,
libraries and coffee shops, appetizers of New England charm. Everything
feels smaller in scale and yet it is here where I am told to take up more space.

Beale Lane, Revisited.

I am no longer the girl clinging to a wine-soaked torso,
legs dangling, feet blackened and swinging around Papa's
waist. I miss the safety of his embrace, the comfort of being small
and held. Insignificant but remembered. Head lolling
as I was carried to the car, asleep, my fragile frame bouncing
against the window on the way home.

Carry-On.

I imagine the flash of sun-chapped skin, yellow eyes, tawny ringlets and shoulders
slightly hunched — the version of me others see when they close their eyes
and remember my existence as an item. I rest in matchbox houses, kitchen table leaves,
and dime pancakes smattered with raspberry preserves. I exist as a pencil mark
on the door jamb in the mudroom. I am
on the roof, biting into salmon sandwiches cut perfectly
into isosceles triangles.

Metric.

I am marked on a timeline of years and heights, etched
onto the white wall in the kitchen. I look at that wall
and match the names scrawled in tiny lowercase graphite
to faces of yesterdays and years-agos. I see them all,
standing at the wall in the kitchen, year after year.
One birthday party. One afternoon of bellyache laughter.
One afternoon of shared tears.
One afternoon.

Screenprints.

The scenes drip in wet globs of rich reds, pinks, greens, yellows,
down my scalp, swirling my vision. But even in the blur, it's always that kitchen.
Always that wall. And always you, Mama, with the pink book

of collected Pablo Neruda poems, the trusted measuring tool, guiding
a straight line from head to wall.
Pencil in hand, you would make the mark.

Tattooed.

Skin carved in hieroglyphics, souvenirs of this place and its people, made permanent.
Calloused palm prints, the misted splatter of half-made love, sleeves stained with speckles
of balsamic vinegar. I taste the damp marine brine of blue shingles and a red door.
I remember the first day of 2010, the third grade. My years will double over
each other until I become artifact, my living collecting
like pencil shavings and dandruff on the baseboards of some home, somewhere,
the wood swelling with the absence of the love that grew there.

East Pine.

If this is all up for the taking, then let me remember
the drone of a fog horn and the asymptotic hum of a car pulling into the driveway.
Buttering pumpkin muffins, their nutmeg breath clinging to eyelashes. The kitchen.
The red floor, like lava. Heat clicking on in July. The metronome of the clock,
its pale yellow face like early summer corn.

Part II

PLEASANT STREET

Doctor Note

The words, they saved me
as they do for so many of us, we the kind
of souls who hurt for fun, sometimes.
Because isn't that how art is done?
To be a good creator, you must be
a good hurter. The words flow easier
from a tap that's been left to its own abandon,
its stream like dirty paint water left
on the kitchen table for weeks, like when
we left town and came back to its stale odor
mushrooming the room, the water-colored
peonies bright and dry on the walls, how something
so beautiful becomes ugly,
if you let it.

In My Nakedness

In poetry then, let me say that love
has been, above all things, the engine of

self-knowledge in my life — and even after everything
is still what makes the rest worth suffering.

— Maggie Milner, *Couplets*

He first saw me naked,
a prepubescent ghost silhouetted

against summer, as we stood
in a mint-chipped tub on the back deck

hosing off the sand
that had made its way

into every fleshy crevice of our youth.
Years later, only three small states between us, still

too much space to give us reason
to see each other. The occasional message

about medieval poetry or our shared obsession
with the obsessions of Maggie Milner's auto-heroine

in *Couplets*. She signed both our copies
this summer. Mine, its crisp peppermint

red and pink jacket, broken,
as she wrote in scrawling ink, *Wishing you all the best*

in love + writing. The two words, *love* and *writing*,
of the same species, conjunct with a mere addition sign.

I am learning both are infinitely unsolvable,
a repeating decimal, the promised risk

of dissatisfaction. I pretend
to marinate happily

into the scratchiness of this discomfort.
I wonder what she wrote in his.

//

In the upstairs corner room
the bluebell girl peeled off sticky denim, layers

of down, wool, lace. Kissed me
in indigo and crimson, filling up

the sinkholes of my needing
with her color, her voice a tremor asking me

if I had done this — kissed a girl, touched
a girl, been with — before.

My reply I don't remember in words.
Only the musked floral scent

of her skin slick on mine,
          and our cantaloupe grins

wide and wondering as winter.
          I never showed her anything I wrote.

What I so desperately wanted to call real
          was instead what I saw in her: The possibilities

of myself unfinished.
          So very like my words. She's back

in Portland and I melt in the dream of her
          still tasting me on her breath as I taste her,

acidic and milky, when I don't remember the plot
          but wake up feeling

undeniably hollow. As if
          she were the ceramic bowl

on my bedside and me, the empty,
          round air of its middle.

//

I hover in my slippery nakedness
          pressed between him and the cold sheen

of the shower wall, the tiles
          mapping the brackets of my scapula,

two knots tying me upright.
When my mouth widens around

three syllables — *I love you* —
the aqueous aching

we pull out of each other falls in cubes until
we are dilute in our own skin.

But I wait until I am alone, steam filling
the shower while I empty — am emptied —

of this artificial stuffing and think about the fingers
of strangers pressed into me. Their zing and crave,

how the pressure of their palms would be easier
to consume and map into words

than his. When did I begin paying mind to myself —
this physicality, this statue whose sculptor I do not trust?

It takes me too long to turn off the water
despite the drought, the price

of the utilities bill this month, and my meager savings
because maybe, if I stood here long enough,

these words would spill out of every O of me
and I could, at last, rest, for a little while.

Waterlogged Words

To ease the pressure
pinching my spine,
I stand in the shower

and steam each vertebra open.
Words fall in clumps —
stream down my legs —

I always thought
they would be pale & pink
but the words, they drop

in viscous globs
of bruised purple.
The muddy discharge swirls

in & out of my staggered stance
until there is nothing more to say
until the hot water runs out

and I am left, see-through,
staring at the mess
I have made —

If Nothing Else, I'll Dream in Blue

I take careful steps on this path,
a ribbon blue and shiny
like the innards of a moon jelly.

A blue I followed with my eyes pasted
to hers, eighteen years of unblinking.
A long time, but never a dry eye.

The blue I tripped over on my way
to somewhere else but instead
found relief in the way his blue felt,

rippled and smooth over the tops
of my feet, a coolness
worth sticking around for.

Why is it I am drawn to a color
that is not mine? Unattainability
makes us greedy, but it's the hot air

caught in the no-man's-land
of my throat that keeps me tangled in
the ligaments of this blue.

On and on down slippery silk, hers
then his. I quench my thirst with their
gaze, feel it settle in my belly, a squashed stone.

Carrot Cake in May

Standing with the freezer door wide open
eating chunks of frozen mango from the bag,
I am reminded of you, or rather the way your hand
measured out five-eighths cup of some obscure flour
like bulgur or amaranth or rice, some bag
of gray dust we had finally acquired after hours
of trekking through neighborhoods of LA,
commercial complexes, and tar lots full of May.
We hunted for a recipe so precise, unforthcoming really,
but you wanted to taste its promise
the day you turned twenty.

So I held your hand as we entered each health-branded market,
kept you company at the granite counter
as you weighed each ingredient,
and watched as the flour and salt stiffened the batter
with each whirl of your spoon.

The cake was just okay
but I never told you that. Instead, I slid every fork-full
into my mouth like it was our beginning I was tasting.
I don't remember that cake on my tongue, but I do
still relish the garnish of you, freckled by summer, our firsts
in a jar on the second shelf of my pantry.

You taught me some people are loved for life. They stay unneeding
like salt that never needs refilling. Thank you
for being a pinch of my living—
forgive me for not procuring our recipe as exactly as you wanted.

Writing About Girls

I am afraid of writing about
the girls as if their realness
may cause their absence.

So I will write instead
about days in mid March
sun-whisked spring
the green of roadside slopes
and Pacific enhanced
by polarized lenses.
We drive
down the 280, windows
open, sky loud.
It all feels like too much.

Inches between your bare leg
and my goose-bumped arm,
Natalie Merchant in
a silver 4Runner
sand plastered to our faces
making it hard to tell
if the speckling on your cheeks
has multiplied because of
the sun
or the wind whipping
across the beach,
texturing the air.
Like rocky snow,
you called it.

I won't write about girls
but I will remember
the night spent
at the lookout point,
bridge lights ahead,
the familiar view
taken in between licks
of Swensen's ice cream,
tasting like weekends spent before
AM flights and swim meets,
years earlier.

Tonight, the hill, the top,
the secret garden,
now holds a new secret.
Her waist and hair
caught under my chin,
who would have thought
I would be kissing
this girl, fingers and hands,
her smell still on me
in the morning
at the spot I used to reserve
only for eventually.

Hypotheticals

If I tell you your voice is the cinnamon sliver of persimmon,
  the little moon
I want to wedge between my teeth.

If I tell you your eyes are winter fruit in the molasses of summer,
  your richness
unfleeting and preservable.

If I tell you this is my second time seeing fireflies,
                                        can it still
                                        count as
                                        the first?

Somehow three years was worth the wait, the months landing us
in this big city but our small, ruler-made world has always been

constructing a home of our own: kitchen sink choreography,
  ocean room,
carrots past their prime wilting in the fridge.

If I tell you I will find you between 112 streets in Manhattan.

If I tell you I will find you in middle of winter, middle of Vermont.

If I find you cross-country summer —
If a video of our legs parting gold grass mirages pings my inbox
  months later,
        then how can three years really be that long

when here you are, your gaze like my eyelids warming in a
sun-wrapped car,
the wind warping outside, but here, you, orange and quiet
and mine.

1/31

On the last day
of January
he told me he wanted
to love me
slowly,
his exhale
his voice
a life then
mine.
The wholeness in our
breaking, what I imagined
as solidarity
in our risk
was instead
a cerulean blue plate
dumped in a sink
and scratched,
its gloss muddied
from fingernail lines
of dull knives.
I should have trusted
the cautionary screech
of metal blades
on ceramic,
a sound so unlike
his words
on the last day
of the first month
of the year.
Newness was always

scary and so
I taught myself
to crave calloused
hands on torso,
his fingers
my skin
as if time was
the answer
not our question,
as if *slow down*
was in our nature.
Now I await
the evening
when I can warm
my hands
under saline streams
of city water and
lather blue plates
with suds and only
break the oil, not
my heart.

Buttercups Never Told a Lie

You ask me how my week's been, small glowing font.
I leave my reply empty because how do I tell you
I spent the day imagining someone else's craving
biting into my ear, how do I tell you I thought I'd like it
maybe even more, than yours? And how
do you put up with me, still?

Today a man bought a card for his mother.
The front is full of pristine daffodils in a shaded vase, and
I find his joy, at finding the last one on the rack,
worth much more than $6.25 plus tax.
The man tells me how challenging it is
to draw a vase like that. He's taking
a community college sketching class and learning
that creating perfected abstraction
is nearly impossible, something, he tells me,
he could never do. This is a man of retirement —
seventy, maybe — and something tells me we're not
just talking about the vase, nor the art, but rather creating
a modern ode, not to Grecian artifacts, but rather to
our simpleness as two strangers at 3pm shaded
in afternoon dust.

I relish the exchanges across the two feet
of faded green counter on Sundays and Mondays
where every kind of life greets me. Where I can be
in love with a man's wonder in a Mother's Day card and
still wonder what's left of you to know.

Eventually I will fill up the reply bubble

with the chink of the register opening,
the smell of an old book closing,
the blush of the first hit of sun hitting my chin
on my way home in the evening, a waxy glow.
You should know my fingers are laced
with that buttercup residue until maybe one day,
they find yours, again.

Aftertaste

After the first boy kissed me,
I went to the bathroom
and scrubbed out my mouth
with a faded blue washcloth, geranium
hand soap. It tasted bitter, the soap that is —
the kiss too.

I shouldn't be surprised
by my habit of abrasing
myself clean and raw
after sex with men, ridding myself
of their want and smell, the kind I developed
a numbness to with practice.
I thought I could welcome a stranger
into my mouth, thought I could convince it
to acquire their taste, my mouth that is —
their desire too.

I thought I could grow into it
like a preference for coffee
or pickled vegetables
as I did after I turned eighteen, funny
how unwell we know ourselves.
Even numbness has its expiration date.

2453 Fillmore St

There's a corner cafe,
two blocks from here.
I sit, my back cold
against the metal slats —
a chair painted blue.
These mornings
I fold neatly
into myself.

The steady parade of legs
traverses the sidewalk —
gray-washed concrete speckled
with confetti of past lives,
all of them strange,
none of them yours.

The legs tick back and forth
bringing with them pockets-
full of lavender lotion,
aftershave, thrifted nicotine,
waffle cone batter.

Sometimes, when I don't want to,
I see you across the street,
apricot linen flitting,
sand-stained knees,
and sunflowers in your hand
blinking yellow
when the light changes.

Her Mother is a Pretty Thing

She wears the corset of this land
waist strangled
        cumulus breasts
                flaunting
        as if to say,
        This is the woman you made.

The magpie on her shoulder speaks in a tongue
        severed
                from the cow's large head
        the rest of the herd
a smattering of calico buttons
        pinned
        to the pasture hillside.

She breathes noiselessly,
cinches the boulder fields
                and wastelands
        around her tighter.
Careful to not bust
        the seam
of her uniform,
                she swallows
        her pleasure

        until the baby she carries
                        moons her belly,
loosens the cross-stitches of her spine.

When the infant falls
from her mother's shadow,
this land will knit meadows around
tiny, wishbone shoulders.

The girl will rest —
a comma
in a nest of pickled words.

And then the cows,
asleep in the pasture,
at her mother's burial.

Good-bye, Maybe Next Year

I consume this abstract mural, your blood and mine
smeared on white thread counts, your arm,
my hand, in it all. Art has a way
of creating itself.

When you broke yourself on pavement
I never imagined my heart could be cement too,
or rather your hands the hammer to splinter its sinew,
red a color you never wore, except when
it came out of me.

In this ruin I wonder how such sharp edges
can have such a circular pull. I am reminded
of pineapple's aftertaste,
the daffodil sweet-tang turned stale
and tasteless on the tongue. I am reminded
of what once was upon
your time.

You tell me you're trying out Joy,
needing to find flavor in your life
now 3,000 miles away from mine,
and somehow those numbers make it all
working out an impossible option.

I want to tell you about my dreams.
I want to imagine you in them
but all I've ever been able to do is annotate
your loving.

But still, we will stick us out in the quiet corners
of wintering yesterday.
I will continue to draft you
in between red lines and yellowing
notebooks, in letters I will never show you.
I will not ask for your forwarding address.
I will think of you in shades of blue and be
the flyover states you wanted me to become.
Darling, I will become the sky and its vastness
you never had the patience to swallow.

When in Brooklyn

I remember it slant. So
Emily Dickinson of you
to crawl up in an attic
too small for your words,
their letters too round, inked
in dreamstate. I can't recall
that night except the weight
of your head on my torso, eyes
heavy but knowing one of us
should stay awake on a subway
bound uptown, too late
in the night to make it noteworthy.
Your allspice curls
coiling my sweat-ridden arm and me
pretending this was our way
home when we couldn't have been
further apart. Our imaginaries
made whole by cement romantica,
this place with a pulse, windows
dripping in screenplay drama,
this story between pages of books
we scanned and scoured through
every borough, all summer. I won't
step foot in a bookstore without ourselves
in mind or the grungy dive
on the corner of Amsterdam, the one
without a name so expect the real deal: You
on the corner reading *Lolita* as if that frame
could swell your CV of
literaturemajoratsmallliberalartsschool.

You, the Brooklyn wannabe,
renting out Brooklyn, the bottle cap from the bodega
still in my wallet months after, where the clerk
asked if I was seventeen. Hand in hand
you and I put strides in uneven pavement
on the way to some corner without a name. Tell me,
did you relish it, too?
On the way through brownstone streets,
the neighborhood beer hub,
the place I leaned laughing against the royal
blue chipping of a mail slot, you peeing
in the shadow of family homes, it was Sunday,
a school night, and we were awaiting
a moment, shoulder to chest, too good
for our own good.

New York Notes

It's summer, in October, and the garage is metabolizing,
its cubed air all funk and oozing. I'm remembering
the slickness of summer, in Manhattan, the paloma pink
sweating off my skin through the faux satin and onto
the faded plastic seat of the B train, where it stayed.

There was lots of yellow that month but even more
left uncolored. So I went ahead and shaded
every chip in so maybe one day we'd stand
in front of a wall lined of bricks and boroughs and remember
it all neon and lasting.

•

By the time this is over, will your eyes be puddles I find
the shallow parts of to cross in a pot-holed road? The smell
of underground city I will find nostalgia for, every stop
a new bubble, none of which I have popped.

I want cheesy fries at 3am to always be
okay, even in a place where I have given up
on preserving the white rubber rims of new shoe soles,
in a place where I slosh through puddles I know
the coordinates of, educated in depth by the rainy season.

Did you know salmon have the sensational ability
to return to the same river mouth after a lifetime
in the ocean? Where they begin, they end. I am starting to
think we are like the salmon, too. In essential desperation
we leave our estuaries to find ourselves made smaller

in pools deeper and wider than we could make single-
handedly. We swim until our anonymity becomes less glamorous
and we realize ourselves are still, ourselves.

That is when we fall back to begin again, to a place
where we first tasted the air. A place like the hairy strand
of alfalfa root wrapping around our waists, between our toes,
until we are bleeding that place. Our lifetimes squeezed out
like pressed garlic, an aftertaste so pungent the next spawn will
still smell its curling corkscrew, ribboning their hair
in our evaporating steam.

•

He says *love you* on the phone
after I've already dropped the receiver
from my ear, so the words echo absently
against the milk walls of my living room
and I wonder into the fresh silence if
we will ever know what kind of words
those were: the 3am train, the steps
and stairs, Fourth of July, striped t-shirts,
the Met, backs wet with humidity but chests
laughing and living with the urge for something
to do, the last night

on the brownstone stoop passing a joint,
my head on his shoulder, his chin
on my hair. I held his hand the whole way home
both of us knowing we had to catch flights
in mere hours but choosing to exist
for a little longer in that courtyard

which had become so familiarly green.
The minutes passed like lifetimes, my limbs
double-wrapped around his waist, *okay,*
we said. A poor attempt at convincing ourselves
that those four letters were all we had left to say.

•

To the girl addicted to Diet Coke
her black silk on a subway platform
primary yellow staccato-ing
middle of the night, the stale scent
of urban underground all the same.
Burying ourselves for fun, like the
maximizers of youth we are, sweating
through minimal clothing.

To the man walking Riverside Drive, empty
grocery bags in hand on Sunday
morning, to the same man
an hour later, our paths
reversed, his bags now ripe and bulging
with the season.

To the cobbled fence
and the fireflies, to the hands
I held and the pink rim
of the Hudson and the knowing that
some fantasies are meant to stay that way.

To the coffee machine on the first day
and the door I opened. The rain cracking

the bad mood of a July afternoon, nothing
like a good cry. To the tears that streamed
like tattoos all night long, afraid to leave
what I had become.

Eleven

The toenail moons are whiter now
and more severe in their absence of color.

At dusk, the lunar appendages curl
over the lip of crimson elevations.

In the red-brick town, I bought a copper tin candle
with the name of an old English poet

inscribed in loopy letters on the lid,
the ivory wax inside laden

with orange, juniper, clove —
New England November in a box.

Soon the earthly blanket of the hillside
will be barren, brittle.

But for now, I walk in long strides up Mill St
wondering how long I would have to stand

under the skirt of the yellowing beech
at the top of the hill; how long it would take

for the color to wash away,
the branches stripped; how long until

I'd be left, shrouded in the tree's shedded excrements,
a lavish coat of flaxen patchwork,

keeping me warm
until summer.

Part III

PIERCE STREET

August

He told me he loved me
for the first time on a tennis court,
my lips buried
in the mouth of a Nalgene, teeth smiling
into the bench-warmed water.
I took my time swallowing
not because I wasn't sure
of what to say, but because I wanted
that lilac sweetness strung between us
to last, forever.
The three syllables held
like the quiet of blooming fog
in the first minutes of morning. The first time
you love someone is bittersweet — the smell
of late summer posing as fall, the ending
the beginning, all at once.
The infinite moments I will hear
that same triplet from your lips,
the same unquestionable integrity
I will marry them with
in late night kitchens and dewy showers,
in the nylon glow of riverside tents and
shore break salt. In between September sheets,
under misted stage lights. On Boston turfs,
between bites of spice and sacred,
in August, on tennis courts, I love you
the first time, every time.

Just Talking

Talk about the sour of nasturtium like it belongs
in a perfume bottle to be remembered long after its fence
bellows and its roots wither
Talk about blue raincoats in the absence of puddles
Talk about mango seeds like shells, the kind that hold music
boxes of coastline
Talk about the fifty-four strides it takes to reach the top of
Mill Street
Talk about the murder mystery that was your clockwork
Talk about past tense
Talk about becoming
Talk about emerald velvet in February
Talk about Midwest airport bars where you mixed beer
with death
Talk about death
Talk about past tense
Talk about nights spent kidney-beaned in the nest of
eggplant cushions, your mind
the nightmare
Talk about peasant bread and honey-streaked coffee
Talk about the girls you didn't love long enough to make it
to Pride month
Talk about holding your breath passing leaf blowers,
through tunnels
Talk about breathing underwater
Talk about night jasmine and neroli
Talk about forgiveness
Talk about penguins mating for life, then etch sparrows
into your hip bones
Talk about the ambiguity of forever

Talk about every moment reeking of almost
Talk about expectations
Talk about chlorine sweat and black lines like religion
Talk about faith
Talk about dimples
Talk about olives rolling off their branches in the rain
Talk about pomegranate pith like extra calcium suits you
Talk about falling asleep on picnic tables
Talk about tears like melon seeds
Talk about all the ways this goes right

For Remembering

If that was no-
thing, then let me have
your scaled hands holding
the rim of a clay bowl, let me
serve myself its glazed arch-
itecture until my mouth is
crescent enough and it
stays that way.

Let me soak in
the broth of earth
and sweet, the marrow
you squelched from your years.
Simmered down to 12 ounces, notes
I only recognize because you've told
me, hinted at their presence:
        Orange, New Jersey
        Manhattan
        Oxford
        The living room
        in Phoenix
        The boa constrictor
        The baby
before your own, long before
me. I taste what I can
and leave the rest to tease
my tongue. I am taking
what I can. Lend me
your hands, please.

Mold me into something
worthwhile like a pebble
I may find years later, long after,
and remember what it was like
to be crafted with such care.

A Modern Awakening

Meet me in the space between
water and slope, those inches
of periphery peeling with salinity,
each breath of the world
a fresh coat. Meet me
in the places I yearn and satiate
all at once, where rock becomes
grit and once we decided to call it
something else. Kiss me
in the slot of sky that swaddles
the sun, that lilac duet
of stealth so we cannot know,
with certainty, when light
becomes air. These days I bite
every piano that falls
from the sky. The white keys
fill my mouth and our teeth
know nothing else
than to sing.
There is a certain kind
of bounty that comes with
sound that is, inextricably,
yours. Not by choice, nor play,
but in the risk of gulping
this happening and not stopping
for air: Toes splayed
in shelled confetti, each stride erased
by the next swell, next wind, next —
In the water I am pulled in every tangent
my limbs do not know. Suspended

by the long time coming, the balloon in my chest orange
and luster, the sun
going on with its tracing.

In Loving You

I spend these days of loving
picking up the adhesion of you.
I am gathering. A basket
I've woven from sinew of the downy fog
of late July so that all to come
could be collected and savored
in the kind of softness
almost indistinguishable
from breath, unnoticeable because it is,
unquestionably, correct. My hands
they hold a hemisphere of blue, your curved
spine and my chest like citrus sliced
making neon out of winter. Our hands
together, bodies full, the word, *until,*
left forgotten.

Expiration Dates

I tell myself I will have made it
when fresh flowers replace aging
bouquets on the kitchen table
regularly, before the stems have time
for waterlogging, when cheery handfuls
are not luxury but routine.
I will have made it
when there is no answer
to the bell that tolls etchings
of afternoon. When time is told
not by way of ticking
clocks, illuminated stove tops,
but rather in the laconic reminder
of canned items' expiration dates patient
on the middle shelf — the black beans
I throw away but never bought, a small gesture
of decluttering the past as if now and then
will never not be filled with one another.

Early Days

Single digits of March and reminiscent of the early days, Sunday
summers spent coated in honeydew squares of light, walking
the dozen blocks back from work, you on the corner.
The early days, before what was mine became ours, before
you were framed in glossy prints on cream walls and your soft
breath strung in hemispheres of Monday. Everything was warm then —
filtered by the kind of shadow only fruit trees
can provide, those days when the smell of you was still
unfamiliar enough that it caught me up in its wake, dizzy
and disbelieving, how now I line my limbs with every inch of you.
How there is something to be made, still, of this air and its shifting.

A Museum of Impractical Things

I go to the Container Store, the one on Lucky Drive,
hoping to fill an ugly blue basket with pretty, impractical things.
The plastic miniature boxes in aisle 2 are 3 for 8 so I buy 9.
Twenty-four dollars, a splurge, I decide I must find a use for them.
On the drive home I imagine plucking out my pupils,
letting them kerplunk in the tinted vessels, like two
blackened capers, nested in tangerine rectangulation. I peel up
the driveway and decide I will do this when I grow tired
of witnessing the world.

On the way home, I call you

I listen to your voice
through sharp edges

of intersection traffic,
tree work, and woodchips.

I want to write it all down,
fill up pages and pages of you

and print your hands cool and olive
on the nape of my neck,

record the pumice-filtered *click click*
of your French pedicure down the adobe hall.

I listen to your voice long after you
hang up, its lingering glistening

like glass beads strung between my ears,
always too much of it to know

and never enough to touch. So instead
I dabble pale pink paper with

curls and loops and lines of gray-blue ink
pasting our lives together,

my tongue wet on the envelope seal before I drop it in
the blue slot, the mailbox on the corner.

In These Hands, I Hold Whole

How many sips of ferment until a lifetime
becomes a year? When
do I forget the hands that held my frail
bones, holy? When do I dance,
not in spite, but because I am tasting the sticky jewel
of summer berry briar and am not reminded
of August? Today

the air was full of two years ago
and I couldn't help but smile
at the knowing of past being past and the coming
home, down the alley with its late morning heat
entrapped with the lust of sweat and
gnawing hunger that satisfies desire.

I was made matte
and unwavering, the drop of orange blossom
like oil kissing my tongue. Today my mouth
knows nothing but the script of ink
left curled around your lips, my fingers
know your every indentation
even when the bend of your back wakes me

and I am dreaming of desert and driving
without pause through tumbleweeds of Nevada
the heat-lightning, beautiful and blue like the years
this moment could extend into. I wake
when early morning brightness illuminates
a room we have made, the walls we chose

to take down, how we give
each other the air we breathe and then some.
I'm dreaming of cold yogurt on the tongue,
the tang cut with rivers of agave like the watersheds
I've held in the lines of my palm.
Today I was a lava stone sinking and burning but
stayed afloat as you buried

your head to my chest and cried. Your tears
as leaden as they get and even though
such sorrow I have yet to know in its entirety,
I understood. How grateful.
The relief. How such happiness
brings the sharpest of indigo.
How you chose me
and I let you. How even in years to come,
I will choose you over and then
some. Our arched bodies
perched on the rim of a champagne glass.
I will trust the bubbles to give us life
when we jump.

Playing for Keeps

Keep me hung in this hue of elephant dusk,
when August lasts an extra two months, heat
on layaway, October in a shell of remembering.

Keep me held between stage light lines
and chandelier trim, you thumb
on my waistline, hickory hardwood sticky
and rumbling beneath four feet, at least.

I'm thinking about how Pine Street has made its way
into every itinerary of my wandering: the blue house
and the pebble-specked car park; the corner-shop-
converted-to-studio-apartment, February in Boulder.

I've heard second handedly the creak
of bristling windows, the mattress on concrete,
the neighbors who took up residence in the used-to-be
canned goods aisle, the neighbors

and their unapologetic fucking; the bike crash
two blocks from home.
I'm thinking about the Pine Street that runs
one way, you and me walking against the current
late into deep blue, filled up with sentiment
and sweat, the kind of flavor I want to simmer and reduce
until it is jammy indigo —

Yes, I will keep this night
and its words preserved in a jar made
of amethyst glass. I will keep it

on the ledge that has grown from my collar bone
so that I may taste its purple and saccharine
without strain.

I will keep the waxy
cherry-Starburst-turned-ring unfurling
on the windowsill, its center opening
incrementally, the red paper roused
from your pocket
of sometime before. Tonight,
the air loud and orange, your limbs
wrapping me in the smooth stone
I always needed, your lips on my ear,
asking if I'll accept
such a proposition of a candy wrapper
ring, as if the answer could ever be
anything but *yes*.

All Said and Undone

You should know I'm done
holding onto bits of doubt like pennies
sunny side up, waiting to cash in my lonely.
I'm done putting in fence posts
for every exit sign of broken.
Remind me to tell you about the spots colonizing
my vision, waking up on the corner of Almost,
skin as aged as spud, realizing I'd forgotten
to clock into the living.
You should know it would be okay if you watched
all the movies first, never read the book.
It would be okay if you never saw the lights
of Paris at night, never took the picture, never belted
the lyrics from steel cut memory.
What I'm saying is, leave the rest up to the mural
you remember your childhood kitchen by.
Pickle the morning in sea brine, find reason
for sacred.
These days I miss dry dirt beneath my feet,
the sound of sky and all its curious.
I am asking you to ask the questions,
to pull apart every word like sweet bread
steaming, to bring me in close.

Notes

The epigraph introducing "In My Nakedness" is from Maggie Milner's book, *Couplets: A Love Story* (Farrar, Straus and Giroux, 2023)

"To the Kitchen for Filling" previously published in the *Mendocino County Women Poets Anthology* (2025)

"All Said and Undone" was originally published in *Gather Literary Magazine* (2025)

"Just Talking" and "Her Mother is Pretty Thing" were originally published in *Berkeley Poetry Review* (2026)

A Note on the Sectioning

The sections of this book are named after streets in various places I have called home. We find ourselves in the spaces we inhabit, the routes we memorize, the street names we remember. The poems in each section, while not necessarily written in those places, are filled with the sentiment of those environments.

Acknowledgments

I am forever grateful for the people, spaces, and moments that have made this book possible. Thank you to my publisher, Dede Cummings, for your mentorship, care, and belief in my work; my editors at Green Writers Press, Megan Buchanan, Rachel Nolan, and Ruthie Bell, for your insight; and all the poets who continue to inspire the world with words. I am grateful for the various writing communities and spaces that have given my words room to breathe and the connections I have formed in these spaces. Thank you to the people of Bread Loaf, the Middlebury College creative writing department, the family at Write Bloody Publishing, and the Russian Hill Bookstore.

To my family —Thank you for being home.

D —Thank you for all the dips in the sea, the fairyland frolics, the blackberry-stained fingers. Thank you for holding my hand.

My love —Thank you for doing this life with me. For your unwavering support. For all the ways you hold me and never let go.